WHAT OTHERS ARE SAYING

"You are helping build bridges and that is a unique, God-given talent. God bless you and thank you for everything you do to help bridge the gap between communities." —*Charles*

"Thank you for the love you show toward all people—it is so refreshing. I find this kind of love ('love no matter what') to bring me more peace and a closer walk with Christ. Less friends, but more peace and more of a heart towards others than I ever thought possible. You, my friend are a breath of fresh air!" —*Niki*

"Susan, I love how you always nail it in truth and love!!!! I am sure this has come from numerous hours of studying the Scriptures. Thank you!!" —*Carol*

"I have been praying for a group like this. I don't know who to talk to anymore. I have been in the closet with my Christian family. I am scared of their reactions." —*Donna*

"Thank you for your blog, Susan. I so appreciate your candidness and thoughtful presentation of difficult topics!" —*Cheryl*

"The world and especially the LGBT community needs more Christians like you!" —*Dennis*

"I can't stop reading! There are a lot of us parents on the same journey." —*Melissa*

"In one post, you've managed to describe the thought process that took me more than 10 years to get through on my own! I wish I'd had this to give my deeply conservative non-denominational Christian parents when I came out to them at age 21. But better late than never!" —*Laura*

MOM, I'M GAY

…loving your LGBTQ child without sacrificing your faith

Susan Cottrell

DEDICATION

To all of you in the LGBTQ community who strive to be true to yourselves, and to the family and friends who love, defend, and encourage you. We shall overcome!

ACKNOWLEDGEMENTS

Thank you, wonderful God, for flinging me far from my comfort zone into a great and wild adventure. Thank you for the amazing LGBTQ friends you've given me on this journey. Thank you for families who have shown Christ's love to their gay kids, actively fighting through a homophobic culture to do it. Thank you for the many allies who have thrown off their own reputations in favor of loving as Christ loves. Thank you for inviting me to follow Christ, not an ideology.

I lift this work in my hands and say, "Here, this is for you. Because you love me so."

♥ ♥ ♥

Thank you also to Linda Robertson and our moms' group, Debbie King, as well as Brad Modlin, Justin Lee, Susan Shopland, and the rest of the GCN Board.

Thank you to my beautiful children for your authenticity, endless love, and profound courage.

And finally, thank you to my wonderful lifelong partner, Rob, who has made this whole journey beautiful. I will love you always and forever.

Contents

Foreword

JUSTIN LEE

In my years of Christian ministry work, I have heard from countless parents struggling with how to respond to their child's coming out as lesbian, gay, bisexual, or transgender.

Many of these parents are suffering from guilt, doubt, and confusion. They are committed to their faith and want to stand for what's right in God's eyes. They also love their children and would do anything to shield them from harm. But if their children make decisions they feel they can't support, or if they find themselves trapped in a conflict between their church and their child, how do they strike the right balance? How do they show unconditional love without betraying their convictions?

In my own writings and ministry, I have sought to help parents grapple with these questions as Christians—but I am not a parent.

Other books have been written specifically for parents from a parent's perspective—but without a Christian focus.

JUSTIN LEE

Now, Susan Cottrell offers us a book from a Christian parent's perspective, in what will surely be an oasis in the desert for so many parents.

In this book, Susan avoids focusing on the polarizing politics of homosexuality. This is not a book about same-sex marriage or Bible debates on sexual morality, though Susan does offer some thoughts of her own along the way. Instead, this is a book about how you can respond as a parent or loved one—knowing what you can change and what you can't, and recognizing the ways your own response has the power to mend a damaged relationship or push your child away forever.

You may find, as you read, that Susan draws some conclusions you don't agree with. That's okay; I encourage you to keep reading anyway. Ultimately, even if you don't come to the same conclusions Susan has come to, I think you'll find much to appreciate in her approach, along with many important reminders about God's supremacy in all things.

Whoever you are, whatever you are going through right now, know that you are not alone. Many others have been down this road before, and many others are going through it alongside you.

I pray that this one mother's words offer you peace, courage, and a renewed sense of hope in an otherwise turbulent time. And I pray that God will guide and comfort you in your journey, bringing blessings you never expected out of even the darkest nights of your soul.

—*Justin Lee, Executive Director, The Gay Christian Network*

A WORD OF HOPE

When our adult child told us they had same-sex attraction, we were shocked. The usual questions flooded us: what would this mean for their life? Would they be safe? Would they ever have children? We truly had no idea what lay ahead.

But here's the realization that smacked us: we were now the "others." Whether we shared this information or not (we thought we would not), the church was no longer our home. In our twenty-plus years at some great, "grace-based" churches, we had not seen one out gay person, nor one family standing in support of their gay family member.

So here we were with our beloved gay child on one hand, and the church teaching conditional acceptance on the other. We dearly love our Jesus who retrieved us from more perils than we can articulate. We also knew we would give our child only the unconditional, all-embracing love Jesus showed to the very farthest outcast—like us. If the church would make us believe that unconditional love was somehow a compromise of our faith, it was that teaching that needed to be examined. Not Jesus, and certainly not our parental love.

The church veneer had begun to crack prior to our child's revelation. Pastor worship, sin management, attention to rules, even the disproportionate application of rules—all this had eroded our faith, not in the Jesus who'd dramatically saved us years before, but in a church system becoming increasingly irrelevant to a world seeking life. Although much good work was being done, most of our experience was of the church's overriding focus on behavior modification; we'd already experienced this (during some marital challenges) when our church was startlingly unequipped to offer anything usable in our time of crisis.

Over the three years following our child's revelation, we met many Christian parents of gay kids, and realized we were not the only ones to see that the emperor had no clothes. I believe God is shaking the church until what's left is the unshakable: God. I believe he is shifting the attention from behavior modification to the profound, transformative, *life* in Christ. That is where our hope lies.

Our primary job is to love God and love others, and let God take care of everything else. We can have more peace than we ever knew possible, and joy beyond our wildest dreams, as our children flourish in God's inexhaustible love for them. I hope you will join me on this quest.

—*Susan*

Chapter 1

THE OUTING

"Mom, I'm Gay."

You want to shove those words back in the box and put the lid on. Your child is gay. Or bisexual. Or questioning. You never saw this coming (or maybe you did). It was not what you had in mind, and it may go against everything you believe. You instantly wonder where you went wrong.

This book is a primer to help you through the process when your child (niece, grandson, sibling, or any other loved one) comes out.

Texas couple Amy and Jen (age 22) had already professed their love for each other before they told their families. Amy had grown up Southern Baptist, with all its admonitions against homosexuality. She was working in a national contemporary Christian ministry, and her job agreement included an undefined clause about "moral behavior" expected of all employees.

Jen's parents were liberal, agnostic ex-hippies. Naturally, Jen and Amy told Jen's parents first, to gain support needed to face Amy's parents.

But Jen's liberal parents went ballistic. Jen's mom called Amy's workplace and got her fired. She called friends and relatives. Then she told Jen she never wanted to see her again.

Amy's parents turned out to be kind and loving, and actually worked to restore the damage Jen's parents had caused with others.

Parents (aunts, uncles, grandparents) have a choice of how to respond to their loved one's coming out. I write this book to show you that you have a choice, and the enormous impact your choice can make on your relationship with your child, as well as on your child's future. I use "parent" and "child" throughout for easier reading, but this book is for anyone with an LGBTQ (Lesbian, Gay, Bisexual, Transgender, Queer or Questioning) loved one.

To many parents, this "outing" is not good news, and you may find yourself searching your soul for answers. We'll get to all of that. But you want to understand how to deal with this now.

My heart breaks for the many families in turmoil, trying to reconcile their faith with their love for the child—especially as that despair is unnecessary. Jesus' response to humanity is completely different from the fracturing response we see in the church and the community.

So I write FreedHearts,* a blog to help reconcile the love of Christ with the LGBTQ community, families, and friends. Because this terrible chasm simply does not have to be.

I invite you to sit down, relax, get a cup of tea, and soak this in. My hope is to guide you through this maze of confusion, past some of the biggest dangers, to help you find your way to wholeness.

Faith Thoughts

If you are a Christian, now more than ever, you need God's personal revelation. I encourage you to set aside what you already know (or think you know) on this topic and ask God to show you afresh what He has in store for you. Whether you end up on what we will call Side A (supporting same-sex marriage and relationships) or on Side B (promoting celibacy for Christians with same-sex attractions), something much bigger and more foundational is at stake here: How are you called to respond to your beloved son or daughter? That is the essence of this journey.

Thoughts from a Parent

"I've watched my own son and I know our children do not choose to be gay. How we respond, however, is a choice. Even if we think they choose it, or even if we think they're wrong—it's still our job to love them." —Dan

*What is FreedHearts?

Let me introduce you to FreedHearts, my ministry to the Christian LGBTQ community, Christian parents, and Christians willing to engage in meaningful conversation. It began as a blog, where I wrestled with two great issues:

1. The great disparity between the call of Christ to love and embrace, in contrast to Christians' generally unloving response to the LGBTQ community.

2. Is homosexuality a sin anyway? Given all the interpretation and lived experience involved, it's an important question.

The blog grew as I continued not only to share my heart but to engage with parents and their gay children through the blog, by email and in person.

Since then, I have developed relationships with other moms who have come through the fire in dealing with this issue on their families and churches. Many of these moms are now in a FaceBook group I co-administrate.

At each chapter's end I've added *Thoughts from a Parent*: quotes from various parents on my blog or Facebook group.

Feel free to stop by FreedHearts to read and comment. I read them all and answer most.

www.FreedHearts.org

Chapter 2

IT'S NOT ABOUT YOU

"Where did I go wrong?" "How could this have happened?" "What can I do to fix it?" No matter how you view this topic in general, to hear your own son or daughter say they're gay can knock you back.

When you become a parent, you know to expect the unexpected. But nothing can prepare you to hear that your beloved child is gay. This is the child you have cradled, spoon-fed mashed bananas, and imagined in a beautiful future. How could this be? What will people say? What does the future hold? You can't even get your head around it.

News of your child's orientation opens a Pandora's box of emotions. Anger, fear, hurt, blame, guilt, denial. You want to shove it all back in and close the lid tight. You might accuse your child. Or try to talk some sense into them. Or cajole. Or threaten. None of this does any good, of course—it only wounds. But what other options do you have? Just to talk about options implies that somehow our child's direction is up to us—that we can take some action to steer this ship.

Instead, we need to understand some basics.

This is not something your child did to you. They did not "choose gayness" to rebel against you, get back at you, or make your life miserable. In fact, it really has nothing do with you. You did not cause it and it's not a failure on your part. Think about it: would your child *choose* to risk being shunned by their Christian family, bullied by peers, and ostracized by their community?

Think back now on when you chose to be straight. You see what I mean? You didn't choose, it just *was.*

Assimilating this news about your child will require you to sort out what is yours and what isn't. I hope to help you embrace your issues wholeheartedly, and leave your child's issues with your child.

How do you handle your own feelings and also accept your child? How do you love them unconditionally, despite intense pressure to "hold them accountable" (whatever that means)? You may think having an LGBTQ son or daughter is the end of the world. It's not. This is the same child you loved unconditionally five minutes before they came out.

If your expectations lie shattered at your feet, then they are *your* expectations, not God's. Let him replace *your* vision for your child with *his.*

Instead, view this as a layered issue. It will require something new of you, something outside your usual way of thinking. You may want to cover your ears and say "lalalala" because you don't like it. I understand that. But since when do we deal best with issues by shoving them back in the closet?

New and unusual circumstances can draw from us new and unusual responses. Let your loved one's coming out stir up a love response beyond what you could have possibly imagined. Many parents feel instantaneous fear when their child comes out—fear for what lies ahead, not only for their child but also for themselves. Rather than trying to talk your child out of what they're telling you, you can decide to be their biggest ally. Instead of pushing you into fear, let this disclosure bring forth the protective mother bear you didn't know was in you. (This mother bear lives in both mom *and* dad!)

Please don't make this about you, because at the bottom of it all, this is essentially about them. *What will my neighbors say? Or the church? Say it isn't true so I don't have to deal with this!* While those responses may be understandable, choose to set them aside. Your child has taken a big step to talk to you. They were hoping you would listen and respond to them about *their issue.* They did not anticipate the need to please your friends, your extended family, the pastor, and all the busybodies you know. Don't let this undue burden fall on your child.

Faith Thoughts

As a younger Christian, I'd been taught that homosexuality was a sin. I believed that trauma somewhere in someone's past caused it, even if they didn't remember it. To my surprise, God completely shifted my understanding. He revealed to me the many people who had a great childhood and yet are still gay, and he reminded me of the many people with traumatic childhoods who are still straight. Studies show no correlation between childhood trauma and being gay.

Please, take some time to talk with God about your questions and let him speak his truth to you. He may surprise you!

Thoughts from a Parent

"Oh, I said such horrible things. I asked him how he could do this to us, how could he disappoint us like this. It was all about us. I'm ashamed even to think of it. But I finally realized (in prayer) that I was being as selfish as the day is long. He was the one having to bear all this, not me. Now I consider it an honor to defend my gay son." —Colleen

Chapter 3

YOU DIDN'T CAUSE THIS

The first thought that pops to mind for many parents is, "How did I cause this?" It's simply been the party line to believe that some environmental factor, parenting mistakes, or unnamed (or named) trauma is somehow the cause. Christian parents, especially, feel *certain* of this. We wrestle with guilt, anger, and fear. We wrack our brains and search our hearts to sort out where we went wrong. And we finally come to realize beyond a doubt that our child was born this way. Sometimes this fact is obvious, and sometimes parents see the signs only in retrospect.

Parents love to take credit, if only privately, for their children's accomplishments. And in the dark of night, they also blame themselves for their children's (perceived) failures. Parents often unwittingly see their child as an extension of themselves.

But that's looking in the wrong place. Parents, and Christian parents especially, can become enmeshed in their children's lives. We can view them as a blank slate, and if we draw the best picture in the right colors, all will turn out well. But parenting never has worked that way.

Certainly parents have a humongous influence over their children. God *sets kids up* with parents to guide and protect them. Parents might have provided unique opportunities for a child who is now a doctor, or helped them avert a path of danger. But they cannot bring about what isn't there. Seriously.

You could never have turned that child into a doctor if it hadn't come from within them—not without serious collateral damage. How many kids have been corralled into a life path that did not fit them? Utah student Aaron had no option from his father but to become a lawyer. And he did. But he eventually left law because he hated it.

On the other hand, some kids (like me) spent afternoons unattended in the homes of neighbor kids who did serious drugs, yet escaped unscathed. God totally protected me, as he has many others.

I'm not saying to abdicate your parental responsibilities, only that you are not nearly as in control as you think you are. This can be a brutal realization—followed by deep relief—to see ultimately how little control we have over our kids.

Faith Thoughts

Unfortunately, surrendering responsibility is especially difficult because of decades of false information that has been propagated in the media. When Jerry Falwell founded the Moral

Majority in the 70s, he began a movement that the Religious Right and radio/TV broadcasts such as Focus on the Family picked up. They attributed (blamed) gayness on a distant father or overbearing mother. Those ideas have seeped deeply into our mindset and caused incalculable damage over the years. But studies simply do not support it. They are simply not true, no matter how many times they've been repeated.

Fortunately, we now have a new generation that no longer believes this, though we still experience those repercussions when parents blame themselves, or their child, for being gay. Jettison those beliefs, no matter how long you've had them, and no matter where you heard them.

You may have to go to the mat on this, in soul-searching and prayer, to come to peace that this is not your "fault." Please take it from those who have realized through long, hard struggle that your child's orientation was there all along, and that you had nothing to do with it.

Thoughts from a Parent

"My son is gay. To constantly wonder how I, as his dad, might have caused this is idolatry. Who do I think I am to have messed up so badly that I created something even God couldn't change? That is ludicrous." —Greg

Chapter 4

"DUH"

When you discover your child's orientation, your instinct is to doubt, deny, question—especially if it comes out of the blue. You have had no time to process it. But realize that it's not news to your child. By the time your child comes out to you, they have probably lived with this for some time and processed it quite a bit. I mean, just think about it. Their first inklings of same-sex attraction startled them. Scared them. They had to discover how true it was. They had to watch other young teens grow into puberty and realize they weren't developing the same feelings. Perhaps they dated the opposite gender to see if passion might develop, yet none did. They denied it, praying this was not true about them. Every LGBTQ person I know—especially those from a faith background—has prayed that prayer.

By the time they come out to you, they are pretty sure of what they're saying. They did not rush out to tell you first thing. When you found yourself attracted to someone as a preteen, did you rush off to tell your parents? Probably not. Add to that the jarring realization that *these are same-gender attractions*—which are almost always disconcerting and require time to process and be sure about before disclosing. By the time your child comes out to you, they know what they're talking about.

Do not ask them if they are sure, if maybe they want to take a little time and see what happens. Instead, consider the journey they have been through. You might ask things like, "When did you know?" "How long have you felt this way?" But don't let your burden become their burden. Instead, tell them you are grateful that they are including you in their journey, and that they no longer have to go through this alone.

Then give yourself time to process! By all means. You will need to work through your own wave of emotions. Seek information, a trusted friend, whomever or whatever you need to help you assimilate this. Your emotions will affect your child, so you will want to discuss some things with them. They may invite you to share your thinking, and they may even help you through it. But it is not their job. Just as you wouldn't work out marital issues through your child (even though emotions about your marriage affect them), don't process all your emotions about your child's orientation with them.

Jeanie was so shocked when her son came out to her that she wrote him a vitriolic letter. "How could you do this? You're an idiot! You're selfish, and you're destroying our family." Fortunately, she confided to a friend who convinced her not to send it. Jeanie is glad she heeded the wise counsel. It took some years but she has now come to terms with her son's sexuality and completely accepts the situation. She knows beyond any doubt that her son did not choose to be gay any more than *she* chose to be straight.

Faith Thoughts

Please do not throw your Bible at your child in a blind panic. Instead, take those verses that trouble you, along with what you've internalized from church, *and ask God about it.* Let him reveal his heart on this. As I walked through this issue, God addressed my doubts specifically and lovingly, showing me that none of the biblical writers had any concept of a loving same-sex relationship. It only addresses sex with slave boys, rape, and temple idol practices. This unraveled *decades* of previous thinking!

You may believe celibacy is the only right option. *Simply ask God.* As he reveals his truth to you, you will find yourself filled with love and peace for your child, and for the LGBTQ community as a whole. That is when you know you are hearing the very heart of God.

Thoughts from a Parent

"I think initially the most painful thing was the fact that he had dealt with this by himself for twelve years, that he had thought of taking his own life, that he believed he was going to hell. We held him and cried with him, we assured him of our

love for him and that we would journey with him. We kept our dark thoughts and doubts to ourselves (he was tortured enough already). I also told him that if he was going to hell that I was three steps ahead of him because he is the most loving, Godly and gracious person I know." —Deb

Chapter 5

EMBRACE YOUR CHILD

Consider the courage it took your child to tell you about their sexuality. I mean, who wants to talk to their parents about their sexuality anyway? That alone takes enormous courage, but all the more when they know full well that their revelation will challenge your core beliefs.

In this moment, your child needs to know they did the right thing by telling you. Even if your heart has swollen with fear, doubt, anger, grief, disappointment, shame, anguish, or guilt, don't let that keep you from expressing your complete and unconditional love and admiration for your child. The intensity of your emotions will recede over time. Meanwhile, your child needs to know that telling you was the right choice, that you remain a safe place for them, and that you still love them in every way possible. Be extraordinarily kind to yourself and to your child throughout this process, allowing as much time as needed for this new revelation to sink in.

Remember, the most important thing is your love and embrace of one another.

Imagine for a moment that some tragedy suddenly took your child from you. I can tell you that you would give anything, do *anything,* just to have them back—gay or straight.

One day, I was nearly home when a red pickup truck pulled out so suddenly I barely saw it before it crashed into my little car, spinning me around and up onto the curb. Badly shaken, I somehow unbuckled my seatbelt, grabbed my phone, and made it out to the grass where I sat and wept. I pressed my husband's number. "I'm okay, but I've been in a bad accident. I'm not hurt but the car is crushed."

Rob appeared in minutes with our two oldest teens and he held me. The policeman told me I would've been killed had I been not been buckled in. I wept, thanking God that I was alive, that no one was hurt. My daughter said, "I was just imagining what it would've been to walk up here to see your dead body." My thoughts exactly. We wept again.

Life is ephemeral, beyond our control, easy to snuff out. Put first things first. You have a beautiful child. Do not let this issue overshadow that truth. Ask God whatever you need to, and let him guide you through this maze. But do not let anything diminish the blessed gift your child is and their place in your family. Now is the perfect time to embrace, kiss, encourage, affirm, and love your child.

Faith Thoughts

If you are struggling with embracing your child right now, pray for God to give you *his* love for them. Your love and acceptance of your child are about your own heart, not your child's worthiness.

Thoughts from a Parent

"Oh, my poor girl. I must have asked her a hundred times how she knew she was attracted to women. She was so patient with me! She just knew, and she had known since she was quite young." —Margot

Chapter 6

TERRIFIED TO TELL YOU

They knew how shocked *they* were, and they know there's a good chance you'll be shocked too. Not only shocked, but hostile. They have imagined you being upset, yelling at them, throwing them out, even disowning them. Believe me, they've heard the stories, and they are hoping you won't go ballistic. They've probably wondered what they'll do if you reject them, where they'll go, and how they'll move forward. Don't think they haven't thought about what you may have already said about homosexuality either.

The risk is very real. Gay teens have been shamed, banished, threatened, beaten, and shunned. They are on the street, turned out by their parents. Some 40 percent of homeless teens in LA are gay or lesbian, 68 percent of those have experienced family rejection, and 54 percent have experienced abuse in their family.[1] They know that once they say it, they cannot unsay it. The following letter from a father to his son remains viral even after several years. It represents the worst fears of the child who comes out.

James: This is a difficult but necessary letter to write. I hope your telephone call was not to receive my blessing for the degrading of your lifestyle. I have fond memories of our times together, but that is all in the past. Don't expect any further conversations with me. No communications at all. I will not come to visit, nor do I want you in my house. You've made your choice though wrong it may be. God did not intend for this unnatural lifestyle. If you choose not to attend my funeral, my friends and family will understand. Have a good birthday and good life. No present exchanges will be accepted.
—Goodbye, Dad

This horrifying response reveals volumes about the father who wrote it, *not* the son who received it. (Even someone who considers same-sex relationships sinful has no justification from God to withdraw love like this. *None*.) This stance can also inhibit the support other family members would have extended. To challenge a vehement spouse can be intimidating, no doubt, but all the more necessary, isn't it? If you are in that unfortunate position, afraid to speak up against the rejecting parent, please seek out wisdom and courage to be true to *your* heart, instead of avoiding the conflict and throwing your beloved gay child under the bus.

On the other hand, sometimes the response is full of love, hope and acceptance, as in this father's letter to his son.

"Nate, I overheard your phone conversation with Mike last night about your plans to come out to me. The only thing I need you to plan is to bring home OJ and bread after class. I've known you were gay since you were six. I've loved you since you were born.

—*Dad*

P.S. Your mom and I think you and Mike make a cute couple."

Your child knows your response could go either way. They hope for love and affirmation, of course. Perhaps they took this chance because they trusted you to be loving and reasonable. Or perhaps they couldn't stand to be inauthentic any longer. Either way, they are hoping for the best.

Quite possibly your feelings lie somewhere in the middle of these two letters. You may not be as fully accepting as Nate's mom and dad, and I hope (we all hope) you are not in agreement with James' dad. Wherever you might be, I pray you can express your acceptance of your son or daughter as a person.

You may not like the sweater you received for Christmas, but you can certainly appreciate the thoughtfulness, time, and effort Aunt Mary expended to get it to you. Similarly, you can express appreciation for your child's dilemma, knowing God is able to direct them in this intensely personal area.

Perhaps the letter below can offer a place to start as you respond to your child.

"Son, first thing I want you to be sure of is that we love you, always have, always will. We are proud of you. We admire the young man you've become. Thank you for

telling us about this part of you. I can only imagine how difficult it was for you to say to your old mom and dad!

You already know that homosexuality goes against our beliefs. But we are going to pray to God to help us see this from His perspective, apart from the culture and the church. I admit we are also concerned for you—mostly because this world can be cruel and we don't want you to be hurt. Know that we will do our best to protect you.

I realize you may be tempted to protect us from family and friends who disagree with homosexuality. We want you to know that you are not to concern yourself with that. That is our job as your parents.

No matter what, we love you and would never do anything to hurt you."

Keep the big picture in mind. Notice that if you must mention your disagreement (though he's already aware of it), do so in a way that *owns* it instead of shoving the burden on him. Always speak from your *love* relationship.

You have a strong child. Be proud. Love them. They have already been through plenty. You have the opportunity to make the most of their trust and come through for them with unconditional love. That's your job as a parent—to love unconditionally. Grace is a foundation to build on; an absolute position is not. Your route to reconciliation with your child can take seconds, years, or anywhere in between. Really, it's up to *you.* Please allow yourself to reconcile as soon as possible; you may as well cut out all the heartache you can in the route between here and there—even if you still disagree. Many parents refuse to reconcile; don't be that parent.

On the other hand, we don't always respond initially the way we wish we had. Many parents express remorse at words they wish they could take back. But please hear my heart on this: your child is grace-giving. They understand what it is to say something in the heat of the moment. We've all been irrational, demeaning, or cruel. They are more than happy to forgive; they're just glad to realize you still love them.

You are also on a journey. You get to have grace and love too. If you have not yet asked their forgiveness, do so, but if you have, please allow yourself to move on. Continued guilt will not help you or your child. Love yourself as you would a good friend!

Forgive yourself. Do not remember things as worse than they were. My friend, Debby, told me she regretted her initial response to her son while she was still sorting it all out. She was really raking herself over the coals for it. I asked if she had asked his forgiveness. She said, "Oh yes. He said, 'Mom, you are wonderful; don't worry about it. It's all good.'"

Okay, so this sweet mom is tormenting herself for something she is exaggerating in her mind, when in actuality, it's long done and forgiven. Please, *please* believe your child who says they're good with you! We can be excruciatingly hard on ourselves—especially us moms. I know you wish you had responded perfectly...we all do. But the grace we need is abundantly available for the taking. *Please take it!*

Faith Thoughts

Only the enemy torments us over our mistakes—God does not! Please don't torture yourself over what has transpired. Forgive yourself, accept your child's forgiveness, and move on with the business of loving them.

Thoughts from a Parent

"As I was telling my husband about FreedHearts, I paused and said, 'This child was afraid to tell his Dad because his Dad is a Christian. How messed up is that?'" —Carol

Chapter 7

"PRAYING AWAY" THE GAY

The nearly universal response when someone comes out (to their family or just to themselves) is to beg and plead that God would take away their same-sex attraction. If praying, wishing, and believing meant that homosexuality would not visit our homes, we wouldn't see it popping up everywhere. But praying, wishing, and believing will not make your child straight. I have heard countless stories of people who prayed without ceasing, and nothing changed.

Exodus International has led the way in so-called "reorientation therapy" but to no avail. On "Our America with Lisa Ling—Special Report: God and Gays," Navy Veteran Sean Sala told Exodus President Alan Chambers of his time in a pit of deep despair and anger after pleading with God to change his same-sex attractions. Sean woke up one morning so desperate that he went to get the gun his friend kept loaded in his gun closet. Just the thought of killing himself made him feel like he was "opening a Christmas present." He stood there praying the same prayer he had prayed a million times: "God, why will you not change me?" Then, Sean said, "I can't describe it but something from the outside told me not to take my life and I said, 'God, why won't you change me?' and it said to me, "Because there is nothing I need to change about you.'"[1]

I have heard similar stories several times from men and women who pled with God to change them and finally heard, "I made you this way." What peace it brings to know that God created you as you are. If God wanted LGBTQ people to be different, why he would not answer at least some of these heartfelt pleas? To leave so many stranded for no apparent reason does not fit God's character. On the contrary, many of these people hear confirmation that God created them this way. Could they simply be rationalizing their sexual orientation? Of course. But as I consider the countless LGBTQ individuals who have poured themselves into prayer, self-denial, struggle, and heartache (even to the point of suicide), with no change from God and no ability to change themselves, it doesn't seem to me like a rationalization.

What I have seen in abundance—more than one hundred parents in my personal experience—is God breaking down our box around this issue. At what point do we reassess the original premise, that perhaps a change in the attitudes of the church, not LGBTQ folks, is required? The "clobber passages" that supposedly condemn homosexuality have already been reassessed and—many scholars believe—found lacking.[2] But the fear lingers like cigarette smell in the upholstery.

Even so, some still claim that a gay sexual orientation needs to be changed—and that such change is possible.

Picture with me the false faith-healers who pray to heal audience members' maladies; when there is no result, those charlatans tell the poor wheelchair-bound child, "Maybe next time you'll have enough faith to be healed." That's an unconscionable weight to place on someone already carrying a tremendous load.

Has anyone prayed themselves straight? I don't know a single story like that. But we know that countless LGBTQ people have prayed, done everything right, followed every suggestion, gone to support groups, and poured themselves wholeheartedly into being straight, only to sink into self-loathing when the promised change didn't come.

On the contrary, the 37-year experiment that was Exodus International demonstrated that so-called "ex-gay" or "reparative therapy" programs do not "reorient" people. They have caused horrific conflict and self-loathing for countless hopefuls, including men who "stepped out in faith" to marry a woman, hoping attraction would come. It never did…but it caused terrible collateral damage.

Your child does not deserve this.

Please don't put that weight on your child, to ask for a change God does not intend to make. Otherwise, to borrow the wonderful words of the wise Gamaliel in Acts, "you may even discover that you're fighting against God!"[3]

Your time is best spent seeking God's plan instead of yours, and peacefully surrendering to the path God really does have for you.

Let God use this unexpected situation with your child to show you something new. He is always doing something and changing us—conforming us to his image.

Faith Thoughts

We often comfort each other with Romans 8:28: "And we know that all things work together for good to them that love God, to them who are the called according to his purpose."[4] But we often forget the next verse: "...to be conformed to the image of his son..."[5] It is never about our behavior but about the image of Christ emerging in us.

Thoughts from a Parent

"I had a lot of thoughts about wishing he'd just try to like girls, believing his orientation was my fault, etc.—but thank God the only voice I allowed out of my mouth was the one that took him seriously, the one I'd have wanted to hear if I were in his shoes." —Rick

Chapter 8

HOPING FOR CHANGE CAN HURT

Exodus International closed its doors in June 2013 after 37 years of so-called "reparative therapy." After observing the actual lived experience of attendees, Exodus leaders admitted that ex-gay therapy simply does not work. Alan Chambers apologized for the deep and broad damage this false hope (of "reorientation") has caused the LGBTQ community.

In a panel at the Gay Christan Network conference in 2012, Chambers stated:

> The majority of people that I have met, and I would say the majority meaning 99.9 percent of them, have not experienced a change in their orientation.[1]

One of the original Exodus founders, Michael Bussee, and volunteer Gary Cooper are perfect examples of this, as they finally left their straight marriages and ended up together.

Later, Chambers presented an apology to the LGBTQ community upon the closing of Exodus, in which he said:

> I am sorry we promoted sexual orientation change efforts and reparative theories about sexual orientation that stigmatized parents. I am sorry that there were times I didn't stand up to people publicly 'on my side' who called you names like sodomite—or worse.[2]

If 'ex-gay therapy' were pain relief medicine, it would be off the shelves with the company defending against a class-action suit. And like a defective pain med, reparative therapy not only fails to help, it can be deadly. People have been badly wounded by the false hope that if they would just pray, study, and counsel, then change can occur. But the damage that comes from that— through self-hatred and shame, through broken marriage vows made "in faith," to kids of those marriages—is incalculable. To require such change is not loving because it leaves the gay person holding the bag, expected to change, even believing in faith that they have changed, and loathing themselves, sometimes to the point of suicide, when change doesn't come.

But our attention is supposed to be on God and his plan for us. Not what seems best to us!

A woman told me her pastor suggested she pray for her lesbian daughter because "God can do anything."

I have a better idea: let's pray to hear God's heart on this issue.

If those within Exodus can see that "ex-gay" therapy doesn't work, why is it still on the table? Why have smaller groups defiantly splintered off to continue this fruitless effort to "pray the gay away?" I'll give you my opinion.

Christians like to see themselves as loving and compassionate, but many also believe that homosexuality is wrong. So here they are with a disapproval of homosexuality on the one hand and the need to demonstrate Christ's compassion on the other. How can they reconcile the need to love people with same-sex attraction with the need to condemn homosexuality?

That's where programs like Exodus come in. If you suggest "ex-gay" ministries as a solution, you prove that you have a "compassionate solution for a difficult problem."

The only thing is, it doesn't work.

Christians want to contribute a compassionate solution, which lets them keep their worldview neatly intact. That's a big reason why it's so hard for Christians to admit that there is no evidence that this approach actually works.

Real compassion means to face what is, not to pretend what we wish.

Faith Thoughts

Seek God on this. Surrender the need to "fix" your child's sexuality or offer a solution. Let God be the solution. What should we hope for our gay loved ones? We hope for them to have a wonderful and satisfying life, to hear God's voice for themselves, and to know how much he loves them.

Thoughts from a Parent

"It just breaks my heart when other moms don't love their gay child...I wish I could shake them and say, 'You could lose them at any moment! Love them NOW!'" —Linda

Chapter 9

GOD'S GOT THIS

If your child has expressed doubts or confusion about their sexuality, don't panic! For teens, many changes are still to come. Let them discover their own life path. Change is an expected part of life. What did you know at 18 that you feel the same about today? Come to think of it, sexual orientation may be one of the few things you *were* sure about. Let your child unfold in their own time.

Lefties used to be considered backward, maladjusted, or even evil—with inadequate mothers. That is no longer the cultural thinking. Interracial marriage used to be considered against God's natural design. The majority of our culture no longer believes that.

Society is rapidly changing its views on homosexuality and marriage equality. Fifty percent of Americans now support the legalization of gay-marriage.[1] This support has increased from 46 percent in 2007, and from a mere 27% in 1996.[2]

Christians are fond of saying that God does not change. But cultures do change and we are wise to pull back from our own thinking long enough to see those changes occurring.

Individuals in a culture change over time as well. We change and grow and learn, and our lives change as we do. Life is a meandering river, not a straight path. Let your child grow without trying to get them to grow in a certain direction. Did you anticipate at 18 where you are right now? At 18, I did not think I would marry, and I definitely thought I would not have children. I'm not sure how 27 years with Rob and five children happened, but there it is.

At this time of your child's life, the sky is the limit. Give them room to spread their wings and fly their own arc. Do not require a certain path. Haven't we yet learned how crippling it is to have to please someone else? One friend confided how disheartened her son feels because his dad will not accept him as he is.

"Caleb will not discuss this with his dad, and the discussions Mel and I have had have been pretty discouraging. Caleb is now pushing the envelope in other ways because of it. I worry about how this lack of acceptance is eroding his strong Christian faith with this sexual identity he is discovering."

Instead of clipping their wings, be the wind beneath them. God is big enough to handle them without your rejection to prove your point. Trust God to guide your child as needed while you love unconditionally.

My friends Linda and Rob Robertson lost their son to drugs after taking the path of "reorientation" endorsed by the church. "We taught him to hate his sexuality," Linda said years later. When asked if she would have gone to her son's wedding, she said, "Of course. I'd much rather go to my gay child's wedding than his funeral."

Faith Thoughts

Have faith in God's sovereignty with your child. Have faith that the more freedom you give your child, the more they will come to the best place for them, sooner or later. Have faith that to find the right path for one's life takes time, and it usually includes many false starts. Please, give your child that freedom.

Micah 6:8 sums it up beautifully: "He has shown you, O mortal, what is good. And what does the LORD require of you? To act justly and to love mercy and to walk humbly with your God."[3]

Thoughts from a Parent

"I find myself lately wondering if the Church has erred grievously. My scientific brain, my spiritual eyes, and my emotional heart are all saying the same thing—sexual orientation is generally not a choice. I am experiencing the sickening notion that we may be embarking on something of the similar magnitude of realizing the earth is round rather than flat...and are about to find ourselves proven very wrong in our previous stance." —Joani

Chapter 10

SET YOUR CHILD FREE

Even more than teens, adult children are beyond your parental authority. Do not try to direct their choice of spouse, career, or anything else. It just doesn't work. If they ask for your wisdom, give it. But give it with an open hand, with no expectations that they will follow it. Remember, they are a free agent. Your love and approval should not depend on how they respond; that is conditional love and has no part in a parent-child relationship.

One of my readers, Scott, wrote this on my blog:

When I came out to my parents, I discovered which parent loved me unconditionally and it wasn't the one I expected. My rather stoic Dad simply looked at me and said, 'You're my son, and that's that.' My mother, on the other hand, fussed for years over everything from 'what will the neighbors think' to 'I won't have any grandchildren' (even though my brother was straight) to 'it's just wrong.' My Dad was the one who finally had to tell her to stop it because, in his words, 'If you make Scott choose between you and Dennis, he'll choose, and you won't like the choice he makes—you will never see him again.'

You have done your best as a parent, however flawed you were. (Weren't we all?) Time to trust God with this child you raised. Do not shun them or take action against them, which will only alienate you from their lives. Look around at kids whose parents have shown unconditional love, and see what their relationship looks like. Then look at those whose parents stood in judgment of their children and see how that's worked out for them.

Instead of manipulating your adult child by withholding approval based on their behavior, it's time to let them go. You have many major life events ahead. Those events won't look the way you pictured them, but neither does most of life. Graduations, first loves, true loves will still happen—will you be a part of it? You still may have weddings and grandchildren. *And you may not.* Remember that those dreams—however normal to hope for, however entitled you feel to have them—are still *your* dreams. They may not be what God has in mind for them, nor what they have in mind for themselves. Best to let them go and welcome the life that *is* ahead. You may discover reality more beautiful than you could possibly have imagined. Whatever is ahead, you want to be part of it and your child wants you to be part of it. Be there for them as you wanted your parents to be there for you.

Faith Thoughts

Whether your child is a believer or not, embrace and love your child—Jesus asks that of you. Just love them and let God direct them.

Trust St. Francis of Assisi's wisdom. "Preach the Gospel at all times and when necessary use words."

Thoughts from a Parent

"When I first found out, I was mad at God. "Why us? Why Jeff? Why now?" Especially since we were in the midst of moving across the country and he would still be in California. I felt like we'd abandoned him. So thankful those questions are no longer relevant and I totally see this as an opportunity to be grateful for all God is doing!" —Mary Beth

Chapter 11

IGNORE THE NAYSAYERS

We all seek approval from those around us; people-pleasing starts out as a lifesaver. How would we have survived childhood without learning to gain approval from parents, teachers, and peers? But over time, people-pleasing becomes a curse. Seeking to protect our reputations will cause us to do things we wouldn't otherwise do. In the end, if we try to balance our peers' approval with our children's best interest, we will deeply hurt our children.

Certainly we teach our children not to be swayed by peer pressure. "If everyone were jumping off a bridge, would you too?" we ask. Yet who is asking us, "If your peer group says homosexuality is wrong, will you too?" We understand that our kids' intense need for those cool jeans comes from peer pressure. Obviously. But what's not so obvious is that our need to save face to our friends is also peer pressure. Overcoming peer pressure requires as much courage from us as from our kids.

One mom confided to me: "I still live with regret regarding my failures as a parent, and anger is my constant companion because I can't change fast enough. I am crushed that the church *is the driving force* behind treating my son like a second-class citizen." The church's peer pressure machinery steamrolls ahead, unaware of the LGBTQ people they are flattening and the noxious fumes they spread to the entire community. Parents need intense courage to stand up to that.

We tend to give our opinion too easily, whether we're asked or not. We simply imagine how we'd feel in that situation, combine it with our best understanding at the time, and offer it up freely. I've been guilty as charged over the years, and I've had to ask forgiveness for my careless advice.

I'll never forget the story I read of a woman who learned she had progressive cancer with a prognosis of just months to live. She became despondent. Her friend said, "If I were you, I'd do lots of things with my kids and put together photo albums for them to remember me by." The woman just looked at her. *Really? Is that what you'd do? How do you know unless you are in this situation?*

Your study group, best friend, or extended family may offer you advice, but unless they're going through a similar situation, their advice is meaningless. Their approval is less important than your son or daughter. While counsel can be indispensible, it can also be crippling. Put others' opinions aside and focus on your child's need. If we can't say in our hearts that our children are more important than others' opinions, it's time to restore our priorities.

We teach our kids to withstand peer pressure; let's agree to do the same.

Faith Thoughts

Christians especially are highly trained to please everyone, from authority figures to fellow believers. God may have allowed such a time as this *to set you free from the need to please!* He surely did not allow this situation to help you seek further approval of others.

Our job as a church is to love and encourage each other, but instead, we manage each other's behavior. Because of fear. We don't realize that wrestling and working out our own situation in relationship to God *is an expected part of the process.* It's how we get to know him (and ourselves) better!

Don't let the church direct your process by telling you what's okay and what's not.

Instead, let God accomplish *his* work in you and your whole family. Let him turn your face to him and break your need to please (and free your child from that need as well). Just focus on *him.* You'll discover peace, freedom, and joy you never thought possible.

Thoughts from a Parent

"The challenge of all challenges is to think of detouring from what we've been taught all our lives—how scary is that?! But not to embrace them completely is more destructive to the gospel than to love and fully accept them." —John

Chapter 12

BEAR THEIR BURDENS

Having a gay child brings a lot of tough questions. It cracks our paradigm. It draws looks from neighbors.

Don't shift all that to your child but instead *help lift* that burden. Let the weight of the discomfort rest on you. Your child is carrying enough weight as it is. They already fear disappointing others. They probably feel pressure to change their identity, protect their family, and fight their own doubts about God's acceptance. Don't press for answers or easy solutions. As with other big events in life, get comfortable with not knowing how it will all work out, and patiently let God reveal his answers in his timing.

My friend was shocked when her sixteen-year-old revealed she was pregnant. Hard news, of course. It affected her schooling and her future. Friends had plenty to say—they always do. But that mom helped her daughter.

Isn't that the least we can do? *This is your child!* Some harsh parents will say, "You brought this on yourself—you take care of it," but that is not a kind or loving response. Surely we can imagine being in that position, had the tables been turned.

Your child coming out to you no doubt stirs up many questions, doubts, and fears. If possible, find other help, *real* help, for yourself. Work it through with a trusted friend, counselor, affirming pastor, or other trusted ally. For your well-being and your child's, do *not* listen to people who say this is terribly wrong and that you must confront your child. What you *don't* need right now is others' uninformed opinions. You need real empathy and support. You need truly affirming friends.

Defend your child from others or insist that others keep their opinions to themselves. Resist turning on your child for "bringing this on the family." Believe me, they *already know* people disapprove. They also know people want them to change, and usually, if they could, they would. You need to stand up for your child and *be there for them.*

Talk with your child as much as they want, but not more. As they navigate the rest of their world, be their safe haven. Paul told his mother, "I had to wait to tell you until I knew that I would be okay if you guys rejected me." That broke her heart, because she never would have rejected him in a million years. But his point is well taken; he has seen plenty of friends rejected by their families after coming out. By staying true to them, by embracing and loving them, you can assure them that even if the world shuts them out, they still have you.

Your relationship with your child calls for that much.

Once your child has come out, you may be heartbroken for all the time they walked this journey alone, but be at peace. Trust that you learned of it at just the right time. As one 35-year-old gay man said, "That was a journey I had to take myself; my parents could not have shared that with me."

Now that your journey has begun, give yourself a *lot* of grace. When you find you are saying things to yourself like, "You weren't there for him," or "You said some hard things," *forgive yourself.* Change your self-talk. What would you say to a friend in your position? "You did the best you could at the time. Your child is happy for the relationship they have with you *now.*" Speak to yourself as you would someone you love. It's never too late to love.

Remember, your job is to love God and love others. You were not told to keep your child on the path of certain behavior, and you will only hurt them if you try. Love bears all things, hopes all things, believes all things. Love never fails.

Many faith traditions wrongly lead us to believe that we can and *should* have answers. On the contrary, why in the world would we *expect* to have answers? We're talking about *God! The universe! The panorama of human history!*

Many people find it terribly difficult to have no answer, but a world in which we *could* sort everything out would be limited indeed. And boring. As with other big life events, we can get comfortable with not knowing the answers, and patiently let God reveal answers in his timing.

Faith Thoughts

Jesus calls us to love each other, encourage each other, and bear with one another. You are uniquely positioned to help bear your child's burden and so fulfill the law of Christ.[1] He never tells us to fix everything—that's *his* job!

Let's all get comfortable leaving an unknown future to a known God.

Thoughts from a Parent

"We have had to look for gay-affirming churches in our area because we had had enough of what we heard from our church of eight years. My daughter started a tolerance club at school last year—couldn't call it an LGBT club for whatever reason. I'm going to volunteer with that to help them keep it going." —Sandra

Chapter 13

IT'S NOT OUR JOB

C hanging people's behavior is not our job, even with our children. The older they get, the more this applies. Don't you know someone who longed to play piano but his father pushed him toward football? Do you know a woman whose father got in the way of her and the man she wanted to marry? My beautiful friend, Melinda, remained single her entire life because her father disapproved of every eligible suitor. Aaron gave up his law practice after ten years because he realized he never wanted it in the first place; it was Dad's idea all along. As in movies like the *Dead Poets Society* and *The Notebook*, this path doesn't end well.

Of course our children would do well to consider the years of wisdom and experience we parents have to offer. But these are their lives. We do not live inside their hearts and minds. We need to respect our children as individuals, just as we needed our parents to respect us—however foolish we may have been in our lives! Did you take a path your parents disagreed with? Did you make mistakes? And did your unique path show you more than you could've learned by doing what your parents laid out for you? Of course! Life is a journey, not a destination.

If you think you're going to make your pianist into a football player, give it up now.

Your job is to love people, especially your child. Let God use this situation to show you what it means to love unconditionally. As we love others, God is at work in ways we can't see.

This road is likely not one you would have chosen nor initially welcomed. But if you seek God, he will show you the beauty of the journey. Perhaps he has chosen *you* to shine his love amidst all the anger and hate (even if your beliefs about it never change). Perhaps he will work through you to help restore his name, which has been so maligned to a large community of people who need him (as we *all* do.) God has a way of rocking our tiny world by giving us quandaries we don't expect. He shakes everything until all that's left is the unshakable. Cling to him and he will bring about something wonderful—for you and your family.

Many of us are used to controlling our world—it makes us feel secure. But you cannot control your way out of this. The more you try to control, the more control will defy you.

Faith Thoughts

Parents try so hard to protect their children from the very things that showed them their own for need for God.

The Bible's encouragement to "train up a child in the way they should go" literally means "train them up according to their bent"—that is, according to the particular way that God designed them. You must surrender the particulars you have in mind, whatever they are, or you're going to harm your relationship with your child.

Remember, each person's life journey is unique. We cannot possibly know the paths our children will take, no matter how clear we think our vision for their futures might be. However, God *does* know our children's paths and is big enough to take care of you, your child, and your whole family.

Thoughts from a Parent

"Become a friend to gay people and ask them lots of questions. Let them teach you." —Linda

Chapter 14

"HE'S WEARING A DRESS!"

Whatever happened to the simple gender differences: boy/girl, male/female? If anything is black and white, surely it's gender. A child could tell the difference. But in fact, gender isn't—and never was—that simple. However startling it is to us, not everyone conforms to a "gender binary," (that is, the classification of sex and gender into two distinct, opposite and disconnected forms of masculine and feminine).

Gender identity is not orientation; transgender does *not* mean being gay. Gender identity is who you are; sexual orientation is who you are attracted to.

Several years ago, a boy wrote to Ann Landers saying he was a girl inside. To my shock, she wrote back that he could make that transition when he's ready. I was horrified. *The boy just needs serious counseling to be told he is a boy, not a girl,* I thought.

I now understand that some people are born with the deep sense that they are in the wrong-gendered body, and no amount of denying, cajoling, or counseling will change that. To tell your child, "You're a boy (or girl), and I don't want to hear another word," just won't cut it.

Claudia knew her son was transgender since he was 18-months old. He expressed himself through girls' toys and clothing. Now at eight, he understands that he is "gender-nonconforming," and with the help of his patient parents, he has learned where he can safely dress as a girl (at home) and where his Cinderella shoes will draw ridicule (at school).

On the other hand we have Marie, who had been severely traumatized as a baby before being adopted. She told her family she wasn't a girl but a boy. She dressed in boys' clothes and insisted on a boy's name. Why? "Because boys don't get hurt," she said. Her parents wisely allowed her to identify as a boy. After a time, she finally decided she was a girl after all.

These scenarios do exist. But many children adamantly insist, from a very young age, that they are in the wrong body and they maintain that their entire lives. Some don't reveal their gender non-conformity (GNC) for years.

All of this can be extremely difficult for parents who cite that "God created them male and female." In fact, God created some both male and female, and some neither male nor female. Some have one type of genitalia on the outside and the other on the inside. It's called *intersex*. This term refers to "a variety of conditions in which a person is born with a reproductive or sexual anatomy that doesn't seem to fit the typical definitions of female or male."[1]

For decades, doctors have been choosing and assigning gender to intersex babies, generally based on which genitalia seems to dominate—though many of those individuals later find that the gender the doctor assigned does not fit with their gender identity. Today, the more common practice is to postpone surgery, rather than arbitrarily assigning a gender identity that may or may not fit the child's internal identity.

As with orientation and other "unmentionables" throughout history (from mental or physical challenges to inconvenient pregnancies), humankind has simply chosen, well, not to mention them. That humanity has begun to talk about these issues more readily does not mean they are more common, only that they're more visible.

I'm sorry if your head is swimming right now! If you have never thought about this issue, you may wonder why in the world I'm even talking about it. But if you have a transgender child, you understand that this is real and is more common than we might think.

If your child is questioning their gender identity, you may experience shock, denial, fear, anger, sadness, or loss. But please hear me: you did not cause this! GNC does not come from an overbearing mom or a weak dad, no matter how many times that idea is repeated. Do not listen to those who throw their ignorance at you, but only to people who understand transgender or GNC through extensive research or personal experience. Seek information from the abundant resources available.

Transgender or GNC is a complex issue and its causes are still unknown. Some theorize that it could be related to the level of hormones present in the womb, while other research indicates it could be related to brain structure.[2]

While we don't understand everything about this issue, we do know that to try to dissuade your child from GNC will only sublimate their need; you will increase anxiety, not relieve it. Only by following your child's lead on gender identity will they (and you) find real peace.

Certainly, this can be overwhelming and terrifying. No one said parenting would be easy. It is important that you respond with love and patience, and listen to their experience. A gender specialist can provide both you and your child with indispensible help in understanding and learning to live with GNC issues. However, do *not* seek help to try to change your child—to dismiss or deny their transgender issues will wreak untold havoc to your child's mental and emotional health.

Andrew Solomon, author of *Far From the Tree: Parents, Children and the Search for Identity*, tells this story on the Diane Rehm radio show:

> There was one family, for instance, in which the child had been diagnosed with ADD, attachment disorder, oppositional defiant disorder and bipolar disorder. He was on a whole bunch of medication for all of these things. He was in constant therapy and he kept saying

also, and to them sort of marginally, 'oh, but I'm really a girl.' Finally they decided they would let their child live for a while as the girl he insisted he was, or she insisted she was, and when they allowed that, all of the other diagnoses evaporated. It turned out that all that pain and anguish and what appeared to be mental illness was a manifestation of the frustration and anxiety caused by being forced to live in a gender that felt wrong.[3]

Imagine if you had to live as the opposite gender...that's what it feels like.

To encourage the healthy development of your child, you must accept your child for who they are telling you they are and allow them to fully express their gender identity. Be assured that you cannot cause GNC nor can you successfully reroute it.

I withstood bullying, abuse, and marginalization for being a girl, yet I have always happily identified as a girl; wild horses would not have made me identify as a boy at any time in my life. This is probably true for you (male or female) as well, because most people are *cisgender*: that is, their physical gender matches their gender identity.

If your child is not cisgender but transgender, please take heart. If you and your spouse can be in agreement about this, it's all the better for your child. Of course, that may not be possible.

You will also want to grieve the loss of your expectations for your child and for the gender you thought your child was. Allow the emotions to come. They are normal. The more deeply you welcome and experience them, the sooner they will serve their purpose so you can move forward.

Please take heart and seek help—and trust God through it all.

Faith Thoughts

Christians like clear-cut guidelines—it helps them fit difficult issues into a box. But human sexuality does not fit in a box. Gender issues, being layered and nuanced, push the edges of our understanding of sexuality, especially when we've held to the gender binary our whole lives.

But consider all the whitewater rapids human history has traveled. Humankind is fluid, and unthinkable changes occur within God's plan. At one time, men married multiple wives—which turned out to be a wonderful way to care for countless women who otherwise would have been homeless outcasts. Not only that, but concubines found provision in an otherwise throwaway culture for women, and God says not one word against it. Adam's children had to marry each other to "be fruitful and multiply," though multiple passages later in scripture prohibit incest.

If we can look at the history of humankind as a tumbling river traveling varied terrain over extended periods of time, we can see how the Bible is an unfolding story of humanity, rather than merely an instruction manual. Our position on these issues must be one of humility and an open hand.

Thoughts from a Parent

"Just wanted to share what a beautiful day I had yesterday with Chrissie! She is beginning a new phase in her life now since transitioning, she is starting grad school, and we spent the day together getting her moved in and then going to dinner. I share this because we were never able to spend time like this before Chrissie's transition and her coming out to us. We were able to really communicate—we laughed, joked and just talked— something I am not used to with her. She has so much more confidence, and so much to share with me now, and I have never seen her this happy—her smile reaches her eyes! Don't get me wrong...I'm not saying her life is by any means an easy one. She continues to have her bad days, but they are less frequent. I just wanted you all to know how close I feel to my daughter now. Once I totally accepted her for the person she really is it has opened up a whole new relationship...one I would trade for nothing in the world!!" —Laura

Chapter 15

DON'T SHAME YOUR CHILD

Complete acceptance, love, and belonging are necessary for full and authentic living—this is our greatest need.

Shame prohibits acceptance, love, and belonging, because shame says something is fundamentally wrong with us—not with what we do but with who we are. When we feel something is wrong with us, we don't believe we are worthy of love, so we don't fully experience it even when we are loved. Shame isolates us in self-hatred and self-rejection.

Shame is the lie at the very root of our identity. If I do something wrong, I can apologize and make amends. But if I am fundamentally faulty, what hope do I have?

LGBTQ people are especially subject to shame in our culture, which makes the whole process of discovery and disclosure so torturous. Brene Brown reveals a particular finding in her book, *Daring Greatly*:

When looking at the traits associated with masculinity in the US, the researchers identified the following: winning, emotional control, risk-taking, violence, dominance, playboy, self-reliance, primacy of work, power over women, disdain for homosexuality, and pursuit of status.[1]

This is a serious situation. It means that to inflict shame on LGBTQ individuals is basically part of the fabric of our culture. "For men," Brown says, "there's a cultural message that promotes homophobic cruelty. If you want to be masculine in our culture, it's not enough to be straight—you must also show an outward disgust for the gay community."

Shame has been foisted onto numerous groups throughout history. Minorities. Women. Children. LGBTQ community.

Teens overall are vulnerable to shame in our highly competitive culture, which expects them to sort out a lot of information and develop a lot of maturity in a short amount of time. Parents have a keen responsibility to protect their children from shame, to counter the shame they face from the outside world, and to train them not to inflict shame on themselves or others.

But many LGBTQ teens, particularly males, are especially vulnerable on several levels—they face bullying by males who disdain homosexuality. They must also face their own learned disdain for homosexuals, and they must face their father's internalized disdain for homosexuality. Parents must squarely recognize their own disdain and seek to dislodge it, so as not to communicate shame to their LGBTQ children, and to their gays sons in particular.

You cannot always ward off disdain from without, but you can provide an oasis of life and belonging within.

No matter how shocked you are to learn that your child is gay, your duty as a parent is to love them. Don't shame them, and don't let others shame them either. You may not have sorted out all your thoughts on this issue, but you cannot excuse shaming your children for any reason.

Faith Thoughts

Jesus never shames us. Neither does he give us permission to shame each other. Many pastors and Christian leaders have been horrifying on this issue, calling homosexuality "a particularly evil lie of satan." To portray homosexuality as uniquely reprehensible is in itself a particularly evil lie of satan; they are without excuse.

To single out homosexuality heaps piles of shame on an already challenging situation, which Jesus never told us to do. If you believe homosexuality is intrinsically harmful and sinful, then let God convict people himself. If God does not convict someone's homosexuality, why should we?

God does not shame his children. Remember that conviction says we did wrong, while shame says we *are* wrong. Even when he changes our behavior, he never does it in a way that says we are unlovable and unworthy. He points out our need for him in no uncertain terms, a need based on our human depravity in a fallen world, not on any particular behavior (no matter how we may feel about it). Through it all, he goes out of his way to tell us we are his beloved. It is time to let go of how we categorize our disapproval, and instead let God direct our children.

Thoughts from a Parent

"It hurt when someone suggested just because our son was 'wired' differently (which he's always known), that wasn't a valid reason to be gay. That hurt because we don't want to discount what our child says. It brings out the momma bear in us. The bottom line is…it really doesn't matter. Ya love them anyway. Don't lose sleep over what might have been, but instead embrace them and love who they are now." —Wanda

Chapter 16

YOU NEED SUPPORT TOO

The more fully you embrace the life you're actually in—as opposed to the one you had in mind—the more freedom you will find. The more you embrace who your child is—instead of holding out for the one you wish you had—the more beautiful your relationship will be.

Your freedom to love and accept your LGBTQ child will help free them to love and accept themselves.

You may be used to having a pretty firm grip on your life, with control as your go-to mode. But you will not control your way out of your child's orientation. The more you try, the more you will destroy your relationship with them. Some parents come to complete peace about their gay child and enjoy a restored relationship. Some parents never do and end up estranged from their child.

Picture yourself in your car with the seatbelt on. You reach for something, and the seatbelt grabs you and holds you. The more you lunge forward, the more bound you find yourself. To lean forward in your seatbelt, you must move gently and slowly, so it will give.

The same is true in our relationships. The more we lunge at them to get what we want, the more constrained we are. Only as we learn to understand and work with our loved one will we be free to enjoy them as they are.

As you embrace your child, you will find yourself in your own process of coming out. We talked earlier about not seeking approval from others, but at some point you will have to say something to your family.

Consider these awkward conversations: "Jason still hasn't met that special someone," or "Yes, Sarah still has that same roommate…four years later." There is no simple answer for you or for the countless LGBTQ folks who must navigate these situations daily.

But here are a couple of things to consider.

First, respect your child because this is their story.

Secondly, ask yourself what you hope to get from coming out. Compassionate understanding? Affirmation? Or simply freedom from hiding? All these hopes are valid, but to expect them will set you up to be disappointed.

You may decide that Aunt Martha, whom you see once a year, doesn't need to know, or you may find allies in surprising places. When Matthew Vines first came out, his parents had a difficult time adjusting, but his grandparents (who'd walked this road before with friends whose son came out), said in complete support, "Well, good for you, Matthew!"

You don't want to tell people who can hurt you by their reaction, but neither do you want to sell people short.

Whatever you do, please don't try to go this road alone. We all need a loving community. Find a PFLAG[1] group, a FreedHearts group, or other affirming community that offers love and encouragement. If the church is not there for you, find community somewhere else.

God knows we all need love and support; this is why Jesus said to love each other and why he has loved us.[2]

God bless your journey and help you find your way to love and intimacy.

Faith Thoughts

Self-righteous legalism has caused more damage in the church than any other behavior. Woody Allen said, "If Jesus came back and saw what was being done in his name, he would never stop throwing up." We cannot remain silent on this issue. Regardless of the dispute on the rightness or wrongness of same-sex relationships (and even scholarly people disagree on this), our prime directive is to love. If we throw that out, we have lost our moorings altogether.

It is in the name of loving God and loving others that we must declare the truth. "No! God does not hate you! You've got it all wrong! If you're a person, God loves you! You will not go to hell for being gay!" If we who love Jesus don't say these things, who will? To sit in the seats while pastors, leaders, or anyone else lies about the love of Christ is to participate in the deception. I think that anyone who adds requirements to Jesus' acceptance will answer for it.[3]

Thoughts from a Parent

"We lived in a small town when our son came out to us. It was horrible. We wondered how we would ever belong anywhere again. But we finally went to PFLAG (the nearest one was the next town over), and it was like water in the desert. At last, we realized we were not alone. I'm not sure how we would have gotten through it, especially those early months, without those people." —Pat

Chapter 17

THE CHURCH'S RESPONSIBILITY

People of all faiths affirm LGBTQ individuals, and people of all faiths vilify them. Jen's ballistic parents are agnostic. Luis's rejecting parents are atheists. Kate's devoutly Jewish aunt rejects her, while Kate's Jewish mother is an ally. *All people have issues, all people choose to love or reject, and many use religion to justify their malice.*

The evangelical church, however, has dealt some of the harshest blows to LGBTQ individuals, and created some of the deepest and most intractable wounds. As an affirming ally of LGBTQ people and a follower of Christ, I take particular issue with those who judge *anyone* in the name of Christ, as he himself spoke only with tender compassion to those who were marginalized for whatever reason.

Christians don't seem to realize how badly their name is tarnished in the world. Most LGBTQ individuals have been profoundly hurt by those who claim to speak for God, and just the mention of anything faith-related can trigger a painful reaction. Studies repeatedly confirm that the culture at large sees evangelicals as hateful and bigoted toward the LGBTQ community, driving members away in droves, especially the new generation.[1]

The church has been at a loss about this. Most *long* to be faithful to their beliefs and the Bible, and many erroneously believe that loving the LGBTQ community unconditionally means compromising their faith. But plenty of Christian parents are having none of it. Their position is, "You mess with my child, you go through me first." *That is as it should be!* Love must be the hallmark of Christ-followers.[2]

I seek to guide a struggling church toward affirmation. As LGBTQ children pop up in Christian families, parents must respond with love as Jesus does, for everyone's benefit. Chanting the party line is not going to get us where we need to be.

We have lost our moorings by obsessing over sin instead of obsessing over Christ. The more we see LGBTQ coming out, especially those who are committed Christians seeking the heart of God, the more we are confused as to why, if homosexuality is really a sin, God allows this to happen. And we wonder how he can possibly work through it all. So rather than trusting God and resting in the peace he freely offers us, we feel it's our duty to step in and try to "stop sin" because God needs us to do so.

As Hawaii Representative Kaniela Ing said, "How many more gay people must God create until we realize that he wants them here?"[3]

We are so worried about correcting the behavior of others that we destroy any desire they might have to know this Jesus that we talk about.

Meanwhile, we trample over scores of exhortations throughout the Old and New Testaments to love, accept, be kind to, encourage, edify, honor, esteem, care for, bear with, pray for, confess to (not extract confession from), be humble, not judge, warmly welcome, serve, and forgive one another.

Faith Thoughts

David Platt summarizes the church's responsibility well in his book, *Follow Me: A Call to Die. A Call to Live*:

This is a reminder to us to stand firm when people who are misguided about LGBTQ people insist that following Jesus is about following 'rules' and that they must behave in ways that are acceptable to the misguided: 'You seek to be godly by submitting yourself to external rules and regulations and by conforming to behavior patterns imposed upon you by the particular Christian society that you have chosen and in which you hope to be found 'acceptable.' You will in this way perpetuate the pagan habit of practicing religion in the energy of the flesh, and in the very pursuit of righteousness commit idolatry in honoring 'Christianity' more than Christ... God condemns the energy of the flesh! There is nothing quite so nauseating or pathetic as the flesh trying to be 'holy.'[4]

Thoughts from a Parent

"Having a daughter who is a lesbian has taught me many things. First among them is proving to me that God makes no mistakes. My daughter was born a lesbian, she did not learn it, she did not choose it, she did not change her sexual preference because of trauma or pain. God gave me a beautiful baby who from the moment her personality began to emerge it was obvious she was not a make-up and lace little princess like her sister. God created her, he put her on this earth in the form and with the desires she still has. God doesn't make mistakes, so my daughter and all those like her are perfect just the way they are. What a wonderful gift I received when God decided to give me a child different from most, so I could learn to value the differences in each of us." —Dakota

Chapter 18

SPEAK THE TRUTH

This has been quite a journey. You may have been rejected, condemned and judged by people you used to call friends, as well as by your church, and perhaps even by family members. I have been, too.

If you are a Christian parent or family member of an LGBTQ child, I understand. If you are an LGBTQ Christian, I empathize with your pain and struggle.

But let me encourage you as I encourage myself...we need to speak the truth, even if our voice shakes.

I hope you have a deep conviction that you are on the right side of this issue, the right side of history, and the right side of God's heart. I do.

I understand the conflict you may feel between your faith and your desire to love and be loved exactly as you are, or to love and defend your child. But the truth is that the conflict is not between your heart and God's heart—the conflict is between your heart and the teaching embedded in the culture that you have internalized.

Listen, if God has something to say to you about this, then hear that. Ask him to tell you specifically and trust him to answer you. If he convicts your heart, then go with what he's telling you. If he does not, then be at peace. Do not try to please the naysayers because you'll never be able to, and you'll only hurt yourself trying.

Being true to yourself is not a new phenomenon. As Shakespeare said 400 years ago: "To thine own self be true, and it must follow, as the night the day, thou canst not then be false to any man."[1]

Or as God said to Paul in Acts 18:9-10: "Do not be afraid; keep on speaking, do not be silent. For I am with you."[2]

Even if your voice shakes.

Faith Thoughts

"If anyone speaks, they should do so as one who speaks the very words of God. If anyone serves, they should do so with the strength God provides, so that in all things God may be praised through Jesus Christ. To him be the glory and the power for ever and ever. Amen."[3]

Thoughts from a Parent

"God has given me the gift of a gay child, and I see that he designed her this way. We are all on the same journey, just in

different stages of understanding and allowing God to direct us as we walk this with our children—not our church leaders and church community. Simply just us as parents walking the journey allowing God to direct our thinking and show us love and grace— it's truly all we will ever need." —Rebecca

Chapter 19

FIND A GAY-AFFIRMING CHURCH

A reader emailed me: "My husband and I are looking for a church that will align with our values and accept gays and lesbians. Our current church/denomination 'accepts' them with limits and reservations. Does God only love part of us?? No! My son is gay and a Christian, and we want him to feel free to worship with us at a church that loves him too. Any suggestions of denominations we could try?"

You and the LGBTQ community are a vibrant part of what God is doing in the church today. Know that many Christians love you and embrace you as a full brother or sister in Christ. Please don't throw out the baby Jesus with the bath water! Jesus does not reject you.

To find a gay-affirming church, visit gaychurch.org. Also, check out welcomingresources.org and christiangays.com.

Whoever you are, wherever you are on this journey, please remember...It's *your* journey.

There is no one right way—and there is no one right timeframe.

It's about your life. It's about your child. It's *your* journey.

Don't let anyone make you feel bad for wherever you are in this difficult process.

And never, ever let anyone make you feel bad or ashamed for simply loving and accepting your child, or wanting unconditional love from your parents and family.

Wherever you are, you are doing just fine.

There are better days ahead.

You do *not* have to compromise your faith in order to love and be loved.

In fact, the reward at the end of this rainbow-colored journey may indeed result in a much deeper relationship with God, a deeper ability to love and show compassion to others and to receive love and grace, and a heart that is free to love and be loved by God and others. If you just stay on the path and follow where God leads your heart, you will find the peace that passes understanding.[1]

And I want you to know you are not alone. It's your journey, but others are travelling the same road. You can connect with others to find comfort and solidarity. Let's walk together and see the amazing miracles God has ahead.

Faith Thoughts

We like to quote Ephesians 4:15 to "speak the truth in love"[2] as permission to challenge someone's choices or "lifestyle," as if our fellow Christians' safety depends on the truth as we see it. It's like a free pass to tell someone why they are way out of line.

But Paul begins Ephesians 4: "Therefore I, a prisoner for serving the Lord, beg you to lead a life worthy of your calling, for you have been called by God. *Always be humble and gentle. Be patient with each other, making allowance for each other's faults because of your love.*"[3]

Paul means to speak the truth of who we are in Christ, not more law for heaven's sake. We can encourage each other in what Christ has already done in him and what he continues to do.

Thoughts from a Parent

"We finally left our church of fifteen years for an affirming, Jesus-centered church. We had no idea how bound we were by others' opinions until we found a place we're free of them! What surprised us is that we have grown closer to God on this journey than we ever were." —Mark

Chapter 20

YOUR KID WILL BE FINE

Wherever you are in this journey, fully embrace the child God has given you and take comfort in these thoughts:

- Your child is gay. Don't be afraid; it's going to be all right. In fact, it will be amazing!

- Your world feels shaky, but I encourage you to relax. It's not going to be just okay; it will be better than okay.

- Your child is gay, or bi, or trans, but that's not all—your child is so much more.

- Your child is courageous to follow their heart in the face of incredible condemnation.

- Your child is daring to be who they are in the face of fear.

- Your child is brave to tell you the truth in the face of possible rejection.

- Your child is strong to stand on the truth of their heart.

- Your child is dependent on God to care for their lives, but independent enough not to cower down to societal pressure.

- Your child has a deep desire to love and be loved in a world that has devalued love.

- Your child is an original in a world of phonies who hide who they are.

- Your child is honest and desires to live life as the person God created them to be.

- Your child is an inspiration to their friends and to me, and they can be an inspiration to you as well.

- Your child is gay, but that's not everything they are. They are courageous, daring, brave, strong, dependent and independent, loving, original, honest, and an inspiration.

- Be proud. Rejoice! You've raised a great kid!

APPENDIX

LETTER TO A COMMUNITY

This father shared a letter he wrote that beautifully expresses our duty as parents to embrace and protect our children.

Dear family and friends:

When you are faced with a big turn you never anticipated, your first reaction is shock. Other emotions quickly follow, like anger, denial, and shame. You consider your life and wonder, "What could I have done differently?" Or worse, "What are people going to say about me?" Finally you say, "I can't live like this anymore, I can't fix things to make everyone happy, but I can tell the truth." That is where I am.

My dearly loved daughter Suzanne is gay.

You can understand the difficulty of dealing with this news— for Suzanne, Debbie and me, our other daughters, family, church friends, work friends, and the community. Everyone says, "This is what I would do." Well, until you are in this position, you really don't know what you would do.

I know the verses in Genesis 19, Leviticus 18 and 20, Romans 1, 1 Corinthians 6, and 1 Timothy 1—no one need remind me.

But because I've never personally struggled with this, I used those verses only to judge and condemn others. I never considered how those who were burdened with this were struggling to reconcile these words with their faith. God have mercy on me. Now I do.

I would never try to change your convictions. I do ask that you act from love, whatever your convictions. Pray. Please do not approach gay people with condemnation and scripture. Approach them with prayer and love—to do so is not to shirk your Christian duties but, on the contrary, it is to be Christlike. Remember Jesus' compassion for those considered the worst of sinners in the Jewish world (prostitutes and extorters). Modern-day imitators of Jesus need to be known for their love instead of their judgment. God and Jesus alone will do the judging. (Whether you rejoice in that fact or shed a tear may reveal much about your heart.)

Faith is personal and no one can command it. God gave me free will, and so as a father, I must give my children free will. I cannot tell them what to think but encourage them to seek God for themselves, as I always have.

Instead of offering counsel, I ask you to pray for us all, don't spread rumors. We have confided in few, so few know the dynamics of this in our family. Listen only to what you hear directly from us.

Nothing has changed between my daughter and me; I remain an active father in her life, and I love her and would lay down my life for her.

May God bless you all and please keep Debbie, Suzanne, Beth, and Lauren in your prayers.

LETTER TO A DAUGHTER

A letter from a grandfather to his daughter regarding his grandson. This letter sounds harsh, but I include it because it turns the tables, as Jesus turned the tables on the Pharisees who demanded "righteousness" of others, blind to their own glaring judgment.[1]

Dear Christine:

I'm disappointed in you as a daughter. You're correct that we have a "shame in the family" but mistaken about what it is.

Kicking Chad out of your home simply because he told you he was gay is the real "abomination" here. A parent disowning her child is what goes "against nature."

The only intelligent thing I heard you saying in all this was that "you didn't raise your son to be gay." Of course you didn't. He was born this way and didn't choose it any more than he chose being left-handed. You, however, have made a choice of being hurtful, narrow-minded and backward. So, while we are in the business of disowning our children, I think I'll take this moment to say goodbye to you. I now have a fabulous (as the gays put it) grandson to raise, and I don't have time for a heartless B–word of a daughter.

If you find your heart, give us a call,

—*Dad*

LETTER TO AN LGBTQ CHILD

A letter from a Dad to his child.

I am so sorry. And I am so thankful.

First, please let me say that it is an honor and a privilege to be your parent. I could not have asked for a better child.

I am sorry if I ever did or said anything, or failed to do or say something to let you know how much I love and accept you.

I am also so very sorry for the hurt and rejection and condemnation you have felt from some of our family members, those you considered to be friends, and from the church. On behalf of my family and my church, I apologize from the deepest places of my heart.

I am thankful that through this journey you have deepened your relationship with God as you have come to know and experience his unconditional love and grace.

I am thankful that you have discovered that the truth of Jesus is very different from the truth of most of today's evangelical church.

I am thankful that you have come to know the truth about God's heart for you.

I am thankful for the love that many of your family, and your true friends—old and new—have shown you.

And I am thankful that you have found a church and fellow Christians who love you as Christ loved them.

Most of all, I am thankful for you. You are an amazing child. I would not change anything about you. There is nothing you can ever do to disappoint me.

I will always love you. I will always be your advocate and celebrate your life.

I will always be your biggest fan.

—*Dad*

LETTER TO A FAMILY

Dear Family,

Having just finished college and begun the transition into adult life, I am reflecting on those who have influenced me and helped shape me into the person I have become. Chief on that list is my creator, God, followed by you, my family. There's an old saying "it takes a village to raise a child," and you, my family, have been my village. I am writing to say thank you. Also I write to invite you to know better the person I am, to share life together with greater authenticity and communion.

I am gay. I have known since my early adolescent years that I did not share the same growing attractions my peers were experiencing but for fear of being different, I convinced myself that I was just like everyone else. I did not really admit to myself that I was attracted to other men until high school. At that point, it became a crisis of faith. My family upbringing taught me that God loves all of his children and requires only faith to benefit from His grace, but at the same time, my church expressed condemnation towards those of a homosexual orientation. In a leap of faith, I spoke to a Christian mentor about my "problem," and he led me onto a path of change through prayer, accountability, and self-discipline.

At first, this struggle to change was invigorating and injected new life into my still juvenile faith. I was discovering the transformative power of God and making decisions to align my life and will with His, so that Christ could live and minister through me more effectively. But as years wore on with little or no sign of real transformation, I grew less and less convinced that aligning myself with God's will required me to become straight.

A crucial turning point came as my relationship with my college girlfriend ended. I had prayed and waited patiently through two years of our relationship for God to enact the transformation in me that would allow me to commit myself to her in a proposal of marriage, but that change never came. As much as I loved her, I grew to realize that I could only ever love her as a close friend. I would never be able to love her in all the ways she deserved. As hard as it was, I realized that I had to let her go, to free her to find the love that I could never offer her. That marked the beginning of a journey of discernment that brought me face to face with God in a way I had never before experienced.

I knew God had led me to a place of self-acceptance, but I didn't know what that meant for my hopes, my dreams, or my future. I wanted to know God's will, so I began to study the process of discernment, to learn how godly people throughout history have discerned the will of their Creator. As part of that process, I surrendered my hopes, fears, dreams, desires, and preconceived notions, laying them before God and opening my heart to the scriptures in prayer and study. Throughout those months, I have grown comfortable with a reading of scripture that frees me to accept myself, to love as it comes naturally to me, and to continue my walk as a gay Christian.

There is obviously much more to my story, including my understanding of God's word on sexuality, and I would be glad to share any of that with you. This letter serves simply as an invitation to begin that conversation, to know me more deeply and to live more authentically as a family.

Sincerely,

—*Benjamin*

LETTER TO THE CORINTHIANS

In conclusion: Our primary, overwhelming, recurring, job is to love. Consider your loved one as you read this famous definition of love written from the Apostle Paul to the church in Corinth.

If I speak in the tongues of men and of angels, but have not love, I am a noisy gong or a clanging cymbal. And if I have prophetic powers, and understand all mysteries and all knowledge, and if I have all faith, so as to remove mountains, but have not love, I am nothing. If I give away all I have, and if I deliver up my body to be burned, but have not love, I gain nothing.

Love is patient and kind; love does not envy or boast; it is not arrogant or rude. It does not insist on its own way; it is not irritable or resentful; it does not rejoice at wrongdoing, but rejoices with the truth. Love bears all things, believes all things, hopes all things, endures all things.

Love never ends. As for prophecies, they will pass away; as for tongues, they will cease; as for knowledge, it will pass away. For we know in part and we prophesy in part, but when the perfect comes, the partial will pass away. When I was a child, I spoke like a child, I thought like a child, I reasoned like a child. When I became a man, I gave up childish ways. For now we see in a mirror dimly, but then face to face. Now I know in part; then I shall know fully, even as I have been fully known.

So now faith, hope, and love abide, these three; but the greatest of these is love.[1]

ENDNOTES

Chapter 6. Terrified to Tell You

1   Durso, L.E., & Gates, G.J. (2012). *Serving our youth:*
    Findings from a national survey of service providers
    working with lesbian, gay, bisexual, and transgender youth
    who are homeless or at risk of becoming homeless [Data
    File]. LosAngeles: The Williams Institute with True
    Colors Fund and The Palette Fund. Retrieved from http://
    williamsinstitute.law.ucla.edu/wp-content/uploads/Durso-
    Gates-LGBT-Homeless-Youth-Survey-July-2012.pdf.

Chapter 7. "Praying Away" the Gay

1   Ling, Lisa. (2013, June 20). *Our America with Lisa Ling—Special Report: God and Gays (Extended Version)* [Video File]. Retrieved from https://www.youtube.com/watch?v=li0dz7oYVIU.

2   Lowe, Bruce W. (2002, January). *A Letter to Louise: A Biblical Affirmation of Homosexuality [Data File]*. Retrieved from http://godmademegay.blogspot.com/p/letter-to-louise.html.

3   Acts 5:39 (God's Word Translation).

4   Romans 8:28 (KJV).

5   Romans 8:29 (KJV).

Chapter 8. False Hope Can Hurt

1   Krueger, J. (2012, January 6). *Ex-gay Panel Discussion with Alan Chambers* [Video File]. GCN conference 2012, Orlando, FL. Retrieved from http://www.youtube.com/watch?v=TXgA7_QRvhg.

2   Speak.Love. (2013, June 19). *Alan Chamber's Full Apology to Members of the LGBTQ Community.* Retrieved from http://wespeaklove.org/exodus/.

Chapter 9. God's Got This

1 *Gallup News Service. (2013, July 10-14). Gallup Poll Social Series: Consumption Habits* [Data File]. Retrieved from http://www.gallup.com/poll/163730/back-law-legalize-gay-marriage-states.aspx2.

2 Gallup News Service. (2012, May 3-5). *Gallup Poll Social Series: Values and Beliefs* [Data File]. Retrieved from http://www.gallup.com/poll/154529/half-americans-support-legal-gay-marriage.aspx.

3 Micah 6:8 (NIV).

Chapter 12. Bear Their Burdens

1 Galatians 6:2.

Chapter 14. "He's Wearing a Dress!"

1 Intersex Society of North America. (2008). *What is Intersex?* Retrieved from http://www.isna.org/faq/what_is_intersex.

2 National Center for Transgender Equality. (2009, May). *Understanding Transgender: Frequently Asked Questions About Transgender People* [Data File]. Retrieved from http://transequality.org/Resources/NCTE_UnderstandingTrans.pdf.

3   Pinkard, S. (Producer). (2013, September 5). *The Diane Rehm Show: Understanding Gender Nonconforming Children* [Broadcast]. National Public Radio. Retrieved from http://thedianerehmshow.org/shows/2013-09-05/understanding-gender-nonconforming-children/transcript.

Chapter 15. Don't Shame Your Child

1   Brown, B. (2012). *Daring Greatly: How the Courage to Be Vulnerable Transforms the Way We Live, Love, Parent, and Lead.* New York, NY; Gotham Books.

Chapter 16. You Need Support Too

1   Parents, Families, and Friends of Lesbians and Gays (http://community.pflag.org/).

2   John 15:12.

3   Matthew 18:6.

Chapter 17. The Church's Responsibility

1   Kinnaman, D. and Lyons, G. (2012, April 1). *unChristian: What a New Generation Really Thinks about Christianity... and Why It Matters.* Grand Rapids, MI; Baker Books.

2 John 13:35.

3 Ing, K. (2013, November 8). *The Senate Twenty-Seventh Legislature, 2013, Second Special Session, State of Hawaii.* Retrieved from: http://courtingequality.com/2013/11/13/ hawaii-becomes-15th-state-to-embrace-marriage-equality/.

4 Platt, D. (2013). *Follow Me: A Call to Die. A Call to Live.* Carol Stream, IL; Tyndale House Publishers.

Chapter 18. Speak the Truth

1 Hamlet 1. 3. 78-80.

2 Acts 18:9-10 (NIV).

3 1 Peter 4:11 (NIV).

Chapter 19. Find a Gay-Affirming Church

1 Philippians 4:7.

2 Ephesians 4:15 (NLT).

3 Ephesians 4:1-2 (NLT).

Appendix. Letter to a Daughter

1 Matthew 23.

Appendix. Letter to the Corinthians

1   1 Corinthians 13:1-13.

RESOURCES

Brown, L. & Rounsley, C.A. (1996). *True Selves: Understanding Transsexualism—For Families, Friends, Coworkers, and Helping Professionals.* San Francisco, CA; Jossey-Bass.

Drummond, M. C. (2009). *Transitions—A Guide to Transitioning for Transexuals and Their Families.* Lulu.com.

Pepper, R. (Ed.) (2013). *Transitions of the Heart : Stories of Love, Struggle and Acceptance by Mothers of Transgender and Gender Variant Children.* Berkeley, CA; Cleis Press.

Vine, M. (2012, March 10). *The Gay Debate: The Bible and Homosexuality* [Video File]. Retrieved from https://www. youtube.com/watch?v=ezQjNJUSraY.

Parents, Families, and Friends of Lesbians and Gays. http://community.pflag.org

ABOUT THE AUTHOR

Susan Cottrell graduated from the University of Texas in 1982, and is a national speaker, teacher, and counselor. She is the author of *How Not To Lose Your Teen*, a unique and powerful book on parenting, and *Marriage Renovation*, a book that offers a unique insight into marriage.

She is the Vice President of PFLAG Austin. She has years of Biblical study, discipleship, and counseling experience, and is passionate about bringing the love of Christ to *all* people, helping them find healing, wholeness, acceptance, and freedom in Him.

Susan champions the LGBTQ community and their families, with her characteristic tender-heartedness, and she zealously challenges Christians who reject them—with her wise insight into scripture, especially Jesus' challenge to love each other.

She and her husband Rob have been married more than 25 years and are parents of five children—one of whom is in the LGBTQ community. Susan and Rob live in Austin, Texas.

A WORD FROM THE AUTHOR

When my child came out to me, I prayed it was not true, that God would change it. Instead, he changed me! God generously showed me the flaw in my understanding about same-sex attraction and helped me let go of my expectations for my child and their future.

Christian parents often find themselves in a crisis of faith when their LGBTQ children come out. They see their faith in God in conflict with unconditionally embracing their child. It's not. My heart is to come alongside parents to show that their faith in God empowers them to love, accept, and affirm their child.

My passion is to share the love and acceptance of Christ with those crushed by religion and church standards.

I have led retreats and seminars for many years. I am available on a limited basis to lead conferences and retreats for LGBTQ individuals, their families, and willing Christians. I also speak on marriage and parenting (especially teens), showing that the great, big God we read about is not stuck in our Bibles but offers life on the edge!

I am also available for other speaking engagements and teaching opportunities at your church, Bible study or small group.

I speak to LGBTQ individuals and their loved ones about unconditional acceptance in Christ, using *Mom, I'm Gay* and other biblical wisdom.

I teach from my book, *How Not the Lose Your Teen*, based not only on our own five children, but other teens my family has welcomed to live in our home when their own Christians families rejected them.

I also teach from *The Marriage Renovation*, based on observation, as well as my own 27-year marriage.

Individually and in groups, I counsel LGBTQ individuals, moms, teens, and families, to provide hope and encouragement.

You can reach me directly via email at:
FreedHearts@gmail.com

Follow my blog, and get answers to FAQs,
as well as extensive resources at:
FreedHearts.org

Also, please follow me on social media:
Twitter: **@FreedHearts**
Facebook: **FreedHearts Ministries**

ALSO AVAILABLE FROM THE AUTHOR

After 25 years of marriage, including a renovation of her own, Susan provides powerful wisdom and tender insight in *The Marriage Renovation*.

"As I read *The Marriage Renovation*, tears were in my eyes and I jumped up and shouted 'Hallelujah!' What a wonderful book!"
—*Patrice Overby, Biblical Counselor*

From a sea of parenting advice emerges *How Not to Lose Your Teen*, a breakthrough, intelligent look at parents and teens. Intimate and relatable, Susan shows parents how to decrease their teens' dependence on them and increase their dependence on Christ. You will be relieved and encouraged as you walk this entertaining and heart-rending journey with Susan.

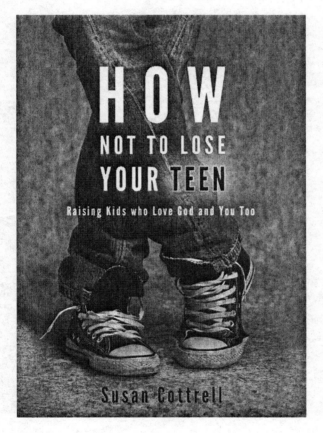

"The floodgates of my heart burst open after reading this book and I feel I have found a 'comrade' in this great adventure of parenting!"
—*Denise Cromer, Womens Ministry Leader and Mother of Two*